Living and Non-living

Is It Living or Non-living?

Rebecca Rissman

Heinemann
LIBRARY

www.heinemannlibrary.co.uk
Visit our website to find out more information about Heinemann Library books.

To order:
☎ Phone +44 (0) 1865 888066
🖨 Fax +44 (0) 1865 314091
💻 Visit www.heinemannlibrary.co.uk

Heinemann Library is an imprint of Capstone Global Library Limited, a company incorporated in England and Wales having its registered office at 7 Pilgrim Street, London, EC4V 6LB – Registered company number: 6695582

"Heinemann" is a registered trademark of Pearson Education Limited, under licence to Capstone Global Library Limited

Text © Capstone Global Library Limited 2009
First published in hardback in 2009
The moral rights of the proprietor have been asserted.

Edited by Rebecca Rissman, Siân Smith, and Charlotte Guillain
Designed by Kimberly Miracle and Joanna Malivoire
Picture research by Elizabeth Alexander

Printed in China by Leo Paper Group

ISBN 978 0 431194 15 8
13 12 11 10 09
10 9 8 7 6 5 4 3 2 1

British Library Cataloguing in Publication Data

Rissman, Rebecca
  Is it living or non-living? - (Acorn plus)
  1. Life sciences - Pictorial works - Juvenile literature
  2. Materials science - Pictorial works - Juvenile literature
  I. Title
  570

Acknowledgments

The author and publishers are grateful to the following for permission to reproduce copyright material: Alamy pp. **5 right** (© Michael Pearcy), **17** (© John Reddy); Corbis pp. **6** (© David Muench), **7** (© Paul Souders), **8** (© Frans Lanting), **13** (© Kazuyoshi Nomachi), **18** (© Frans Lanting), **20 TR** (© Rainer Hackenberg/zefa), **21 BR** (© Elio Ciol); Getty Images pp.**11** (Eastcott Momatiuk/Photographer's Choice), **12** (Joel Sartore/National Geographic); Photolibrary pp.**4** (Otto Hahn/Picture Press), **15** (Rodger Jackman/ OSF), **16** (Gabriela Staebler/Cusp), **19** (Michael Fogden/OSF), **20 BR** (Chad Ehlers); Shutterstock pp.**5 left** (© Maksym Gorpenyuk), **9** (© Elisei Shafer), **10** (© Steve Estvanik), **14** (© ANP), **20 BL** (© Leighton Photography & Imaging), **20 TL** (© javarman), **21 BL** (© Hiroshi Sato), **21 TL** (© ciapix), **21 TR** (© Mario Bruno).

Cover photograph of a chameleon reproduced with permission of Corbis/ © Frans Lemmens/zefa/. Back cover photograph reproduced with permission of Shutterstock (© Hiroshi Sato).

We would like to thank Nancy Harris and Adriana Scalise for their help in the preparation of this book.

Every effort has been made to contact copyright holders of any material reproduced in this book. Any omissions will be rectified in subsequent printings if notice is given to the publisher.

Contents

Some words are shown in bold, **like this**. They are explained in "Words to know" on page 23.

Living things

Living things are alive. Living things grow.
Plants and animals are living things. Living things
have needs.

Animals need **air**, food, and water so they can stay alive. Plants need air, light, water, and **nutrients** so they can stay alive.

Non-living things

Non-living things are not alive. Non-living things do not grow and do not have needs.

Non-living things do not need food or water.
Non-living things do not need **air**, light, or **nutrients**.

Habitats

A **habitat** is a place where certain types of plants or animals live. There are many different habitats on Earth.

In each habitat, there are living and non-living things. Can you tell which things are living and which things are non-living in each of the habitats in this book?

Polar habitats

Polar habitats are areas of land and water near the **North Pole** and the **South Pole**. Polar habitats are very cold. There are many living and non-living things in a polar habitat.

This seal is in a polar habitat. Is it living or non-living? Does it need food, **air**, and water? Does it grow?

The seal is living!

Desert

Deserts are areas of dry land. It can be very hot in a desert. There are many living and non-living things in a desert **habitat**.

This sand is in a desert habitat. Is it living or non-living? Does sand need **air**, food, and water? Does it grow?

The sand is non-living!

Ocean

Oceans are very large areas of water. There are many living and non-living things in an ocean **habitat**.

This lobster is in an ocean habitat. Is it living or
non-living? Does it need **air**, food, and water?
Does it grow?

This lobster is living!

Grassland

Grasslands are open areas of land with few trees. There are many living and non-living things in a grassland **habitat**.

This **pond** is in a grassland habitat. Is it living or non-living? Does it need **air**, water, and food? Does it grow?

This pond is non-living!

Rainforest

Rainforests are large forests that grow in warm, wet weather. There are many living and non-living things in a rainforest **habitat**.

This plant is in a rainforest habitat. Is it living or non-living? Does it need **air**, light, water, and **nutrients**? Does it grow?

This plant is living!

Living or non-living?

rock

plant

snake

waterfall

Which of these things are living and which of these things are non-living? Turn to page 22 to find out.

snow

palm tree

dolphin

stream

Find out!

The rock is **non-living**.

The plant is **living**.

The snake is **living**.

The waterfall is **non-living**.

The snow is **non-living**.

The palm tree is **living**.

The dolphin is **living**.

The stream is **non-living**.

Words to know

air gas that plants and animals need to take in to stay alive. We cannot see the air but it is all around us on Earth.

desert area of dry land. Deserts are usually very hot during the day and cold at night.

grassland an area of land with a lot of grass and few trees

habitat a place where particular kinds of plants grow and particular kinds of animals live. A forest, a desert, and an ocean are all examples of different habitats.

North Pole place on Earth that is as far north as you can go. The weather is very cold at the North Pole.

nutrients things often found in the soil that plants need to stay healthy

ocean large area of water

polar area around the North Pole or the South Pole

pond a small area of water

rainforest forest in places where the weather is usually very hot and wet

South Pole place on Earth that is as far south as you can go. The weather is very cold at the South Pole.

Index

Notes for parents and teachers

Before reading

Show the children pictures of several things that are living. Ask what the living things have in common and what they need. Talk about living things needing food, water, and air. Show pictures of non-living things. Ask what the non-living things have in common. Explain that non-living things do not need air, food, or water. Tell children that a place where certain plants and animals live is called a habitat. Explain that we can find both living and non-living things in each habitat.

After reading

Collect four to six pictures from each habitat (desert, polar, rainforest, grassland, and ocean). The pictures should be of both living and non-living things. Put pictures from each individual habitat in a plastic bag or envelope and label it with the name of the habitat. Use the envelopes for the activities below.

• Give children one or two envelopes and ask them to sort the pictures into living and non-living things. Ask them why they sorted the pictures in the way that they did.

• Give children two, three, or four envelopes. Ask them to mix up the pictures, and then sort the pictures by habitats.

• Once the pictures have been sorted, the children can glue them down on a piece of paper grouped either by living and non-living things or by habitat.